OUT (

BUTTERFLY MIND

A selection of poems

from heartfelt to humorous

and

from traditional to free verse

by

JANET TURNER

Janet Turner

First published in Great Britain in 2014.

This edition published by skoobebooks 2017.

Available from www.skoobebooks.co.uk/book-shop/, Amazon and other book-selling websites.

OUT OF MY BUTTERFLY MIND

This collection of poems reflects my journey as I write about things that I love, places that inspire me, thoughts on life and death, and things that make me laugh.

My aim is to provide a selection of traditional and modern poetry that is enjoyable and, above all, easy to comprehend.

I do not claim to be a great poet and as you will see, if you progress beyond the first page, my butterfly mind flits between serious and just plain silly.

Come, travel with me on my Butterfly flight.

Janet Turner

Janet can be contacted via e-mail at janetturner335@gmail.com.

CONTENTS

Shakespearean Sonnet

NEW FOREST SUNRISE

As summer sunrise sweeps away
the mournful mist across the plain
warm golden light renews the day
revealing trees refreshed by rain.
Here, ancient oaks and stately beech
stretch up in splendour to the sky
while shining birches gently reach
their whispering silver branches high.
Stepping quietly to a stream
the gentle Fallow brings her fawn.
Then, like a fairy-tale, they seem
to vanish in the lightening dawn.
If only I could start each day
in such a peaceful, joyful way.

Shakespearean Sonnet

NEW FOREST AUTUMN

Beneath my feet the damp earth gently gives
a sigh of mossy breath and toadstool dreams.
Through golden leaves the Autumn sunlight sieves
cascading down in multi-coloured beams.
The robin still sings from his perch on high
forgetting that his nestlings have all flown,
while high above I hear a buzzard's cry
describing lofty circles on his own.
But now, within the Forest, comes the sound
of roars reverberating through the trees
as red stags struggle to maintain their ground
and bring each weaker rival to its knees.
Yet from this savage battle will be born
next spring another gentle, doe-eyed fawn.

A Terza Rima

THE KING STAG

As early morning mist swirls round the trees,
soft silhouettes against the brightening sky,
I walk through heather's purple swaying seas

hoping to hear that wild and savage cry
as red deer gather for their autumn tryst,
the great stags strutting, roaring to defy

all rivals hidden by the clinging mist.
At last the king stag steps out on the plain,
great spreading antlers morning sunlight kissed.

The champion last year, he comes again,
his lion-roars the loudest and the best.
Once more he finds no challengers remain

who'd dare engage their antlers in the test
to win the right to gather hinds and mate.
The king stag rules supreme above the rest.

Next year, perhaps, another just as great
will send the old king to his weary fate.

NEW FOREST SANCTUARY

In search of solitude, I seek refuge
here in the shade of ancient oaks,
listening to their slow heartbeat
unceasing for centuries.
Their calm strength comforts me,
offers me the joy of their beauty.

Walking through a cathedral
of tall, elegant beeches,
humbled by their soaring trunks,
my troubles sink to nothingness
and peace fills my heart.
The forest works its magic.

Then out into the sunshine
of the open, heathery moor
where soaring woodlarks lift
their spring-songs to the sky,
and peaceful ponies wander
heavy with unborn foals.

I follow a shallow stream
back into cool forest shade
where I can sit and watch
the shy deer drinking their reflections.
Diamonds drip from their lips
as they tiptoe gently away.

I return home renewed and refreshed
ready again to face daily life.
Problems recede before my new strength
and vanish into the moorland mist.
My haven, my comfort, this wonderful place
will never leave my heart.

BARKING (or Rhymed to Death)

Don't mess with me — I'm the biggest tree
in this wood. Understood?
I'm no alder that creeps or willow that weeps
hanging her head in a stream,
or a gangling beech trying to reach
to the sky, an impossible dream.

Lift up your head, admire my spread,
I tell you, my heartwood is good
for two centuries more, while unfortunately your
brief life will soon stop, you are due for the chop,
a fate you deserve, as you've had the nerve
to carve in my bark — now just stop!

I think you should know that a long time ago
your people came here, in awe and in fear.
They crept through the trees and got down on their knees
to worship my strength and my size.
Therefore I still expect you to show me respect,
it's time for a new sacrifice.

The man wondered how he was struck by a bough
felling him to the ground, and the very last sound
the tree's victim heard was the song of a bird
and the whisper of leaves dropping down from the trees.
As he lay in the mud, his sacrificed blood
paid the price for his thoughtless misdeeds.

TEACHER, TEACHER

Teacher, Teacher, burning bright
is it possible I might
avoid rejection and removal,
even meet with your approval,
if I get my classwork right?

THE ARTIST

I'm a budding artist
out amongst the greenery
alone and blissfully absorbed
painting all the scenery.

But the gods don't like me
so I'm not doing well,
and soon my peaceful hideaway
is somewhere more like hell.

There's things that buzz around me
or drop into my hair,
and Oh, what purgatory –
PEOPLE COME AND STARE!

'Minute' Poem as originated by Verna Lee Hinegardner of Arkansas

THE LONG VIEW

Our orbit spins us far above
the Earth we love.
We gaze in awe
as sea and shore
revolve in shades of blue and white –
breath-taking sight.
From this high place
we see no trace
of vicious wars that rage below.
It is as though
this heavenly peace
has made wars cease.

WASTING TIME

Of all the bloody silly ways
to spend my days,
there's nothing worse
than writing verse
that with iambic metre goes
right up my nose.
With eight beats here,
then four, I fear
that my poor brain just cannot cope –
I've lost all hope.
I'd like to see
this Verna Lee!

Shakespearean Sonnet

HOLIDAY ROMANCE

Enshrouded in a heavy Highland mist
the Scottish hills are where I lost my heart.
At dawning day we slowly walked and kissed,
only to learn next day we'd have to part.
For you, your call-up papers claimed your life
and took you from me far across the sea.
Two years before you'd claim me as your wife
when finally the Army set you free.
How quickly, then, the busy years flew by
in whirls of work and setting up a home.
Two children raised, until prepared to fly
and find their own way through this world to roam.
And friends' advice comes to me come to me from the past —
a holiday romance will never last!

Unrhymed Couplets

TROSSACHS ROMANCE

We wandered through the forest as the blushing spring-time dawn
smiled shyly through the trees beside the loch.

Together we stepped softly, holding new-met hands,
through a misty, shifting world of half-seen dreams.

Shafts of golden sunlight blessed Ben Lomond's lofty head
while pink clouds sailed beneath us in Loch Ard.

We turned and kissed each other, vowing to return
at some time in the future to this special, mystic place.

After fifty years of marriage we are standing here again,
this time to watch the startling evening sky.

The blazing reds and golds turn to silver, like our hair,
in cold reflections showing we've grown old.

Content with our last visit to this land where we first met
we'll take these memories southwards to our home.

Petrarchan Sonnet

DOWNLAND INHERITANCE

The South Downs rise and fall like wind-blown waves
crested with turf, sweet-smelling and serene,
where evening shadows curl and creep between
the mounds that cover ancient warriors' graves.
Their bones aligned with shields and spears and staves,
they sleep secure where twisted hawthorns lean
and drop white blossom on the battle scene.
They laid their lives down rather than be slaves.
Our fathers, too, fought for the right to dwell
in freedom, grazing sheep upon these hills
where, still, the skylark serenades the sky.
Away from cities' traffic-roaring hell
and modern mankind's frantic search for thrills
I'll rest, content and peaceful, 'til I die.

SHADE ON THE DOWNS

In summer heat I climbed the hill
dazzled by the sunlight's glare.
Midge tormented, hot, but still
determined that I *would* get there.

The sunburnt turf beneath my feet
was brown as last year's crop of hay.
No green, thyme-scented herbage sweet
to cheer and soothe me on my way.

And then, this pilgrim's final goal
atop the shimmering, whale-backed Down,
salvation for my weary soul —
beech trees formed into a crown.

Cathedral-like, with sturdy limbs
raised in silent, sombre prayer,
their shade held echoes of the hymns
once sung by ancient people there.

I entered quietly, half afraid
my presence may disturb the peace
of this cooling, calming shade
bestowed as blessing by the trees.

I sank down on a log and there
reviewed my life, my hopes, my fears,
and offered up a grateful prayer
for family love throughout the years.

I spoke to God there in the trees,
not in a church with pomp and show,
not even down upon my knees –
He listened, and He heard, I know.

STATIC

Crowning a steep-sided Downland hill
a stately stand of wind-sculptured oaks
gazed patiently down at the low Weald.
Thankfully sinking into their shade
I rested at their mossy, gnarled feet,
and I, too, observed the world below.

A village busy with tourist cars
like bees buzzing round a flower-bed.
A distant by-pass, whose muted roar
told tales of urgent deliveries.
An aircraft, wingtips scratching the sky,
its vapour trail shining in the sun,
carrying people across the world.

"How sad," I murmured to the old trees,
"to be earth-tied to only one place,
unable to move, to walk, explore.
Just think what wonderful things you'd see."

"Fool!" said the trees, with their rustling leaves,
"passing centuries increase our strength.
We watch and we wait, while mankind's fate
is to breed and die. Poor butterfly —
when you're gone, we'll be standing here still."

A Terza Rima

SPRING MAGIC

There is magic in the misty dawning
of early springtime's longed-for soft return.
Vague shapes reach out to welcome a new morning

revealing hillsides where the sun's rays burn
away the shrouds of moisture from tall trees
and green emerging fronds of fragile fern.

A placid cow lifts up her head and sees
the ghosting barn owl quartering the ground.
Merging with the mist she hunts with ease

across the fields where mice and voles are found.
But soon the sun's warmth spreads its golden light
and ringing through the valley comes the sound

of songbirds welcoming the end of night,
a glorious song that puts the cold to flight.

RED WELLIES

Our son’s first wellies,
bright red, irresistible.
His puzzled eyes look down
at these new, sturdy feet.
“What are these?
Where are we going?”

In cool depths of forest
we find a small stream
with inviting gravel shallows
and deeper, dark pools.

Wobbling and wondering,
holding Daddy’s hand,
he toddles to the edge.
“Can I really?”
Delight tinged with fear —
such a big adventure.

A few gentle splashes, a chuckle, a jump,
a diamond-sprayed run into a deep pool.
He finds a small stick, launches it,
watches its journey downstream.

At last, wet and protesting,
we retrieve the budding naval captain,
with assurances of an early return.
Our laughter flows with the stream
as we sit on the bank and empty the wellies,
pouring a libation to the water nymphs.

GRANDFATHER'S BENCH

Inherited, neglected, battered by wind and weather,
the old garden bench waits patiently for spring.
Wooden struts open their rough skins,
chapped into splinters, drying to death.

Touched by the tip of a tentative finger
a wooden arm scratches in self-defence.
I am accused before the bench of cruel neglect,
failure to feed and nourish its timber.

The birds, the flowers, the fish in the pond
are tended with care and devotion
but the sturdy bench patiently stands
decaying like an unwanted pensioner.

At last, guilty as charged, I kneel at its feet
brushing away the collected grime
then anointing with oil the creaking limbs
in humble supplication.

Recovery is slow as the weather warms
and tempts me to sit in the garden.
I relax on the seat that my Grandfather loved,
welcomed by his warm embrace.

NO APPRECIATION

A blackbird perches on my garden shed,
yellow beak raised like a conductor's baton.
Glorious notes of his challenging song
spill across the flower beds.

Incandescent bubbles of joy
float in the sunlight.
I am enraptured, inspired.
What music! What enchantment!

My soul absorbs the sweet-sounding notes
and my mouth opens in response
to add my voice to his in harmony
with a springtime serenade.

He glares, stops singing,
dives over my washing line.
Swoop, poop –
he's squitted on my sheets.
No appreciation!

VISIT OF THE EMPEROR

Lazily watching my fish
fumbling for food, overfed,
quick movement catches my eye,
there, here, over the surface.

Flash of green and startling blue
as a dragonfly quarters the pond
flying faster than his reflection,
or so it seems.

Dry wings crackle with speed,
powered by massive thorax muscles,
as the Emperor seeks out his prey
with such incredible skill.

Rising suddenly to my face
he helicopters with ease,
faceted eyes staring into mine.
How many of me does he see?

Flicker, flash, this flying jewel
resumes his dashing aerial display,
reactions so fast, his turns so quick
I am humbled by his skill.

Hard to believe that once he lived
as an ugly monster in this very pond.
Crawling through mud, with extending jaws
that were still fast enough to kill.

Does he remember his former life?
Years spent away from the sun?
Released from the depths, he now appears
drunk with the joy of his flight.

I stand there, entranced, watching his dance
as the warm summer evening draws in.
The whir of his wings rustles past,
a quick flash of colour — he's gone.

LIMERICKS

There was a young sailor from Dover
who was known as a bit of a rover,
until wife number three
said 'Come, walk with me
on the cliff top,' and pushed him right over.

A misguided man from Dunoon
said he wanted to fly to the moon.
He bought a large rocket,
put it in his back pocket –
he's been up in orbit since June.

Acrostic Poems (using the word Creative)

ARTISTIC

Contemplating the model's pose,
Rearranging each elegant limb,
Every angle of cheek and nose
Assessed until all appears to him
To make just the picture that he had in mind.
It must be completed and placed in a frame
Viewed by the critics, who'll hopefully find
Exceptional talent, leading to fame.

INHERITED TALENT

Collecting our son at the end of the day,
Rushing and stressed, I arrive rather late.
Exploding with joy, he rushes my way
And jumps in my arms as I wait at the gate.
"**T**oday I've done something real special for you,
I've maded a monster wiv big snappy jaws."
Viewing his offering of paper and glue
Explains gene inheritance – definitely yours!

Narrative Poem

THE CRISIS

My anxious ears are straining for the ringing of the bell,
the door is left unlatched to let them in.
Their beds are made up ready, and as far as I can tell
my house is clean and shiny as a pin.

I've climbed into the attic – that's not easy at my age –
dug out the rusty trunk full of old toys.
There's a lovely wooden farmyard, and a parrot in a cage
which mechanically moves and makes a noise.

I've found a pretty dolly with a frilly, flouncy dress
that I'm sure will please young Lynne, who's nearly six,
and a teddy with one eye, grunty-growling when you press
his tummy-button hard (it sometimes sticks).

Young Ben is only four, but I'm reasonably sure
that my son's old train set will be lots of fun.
I've laid the tracks out neatly, spreading right across the floor –
I'm just hoping that the engines will still run.

Now, suddenly they're here, as I hear excited cries —
the garden gate goes bang against the fence,
and following the children, with worry-wounded eyes,
comes their Daddy, looking weary, gaunt and tense.

"Granny Seaside!" shriek the children, completely unaware,
as they race hip-hopping happily within.
Gangly, girly little Lynne with her bouncy, blonde-curled hair,
and sturdy Ben aglow with cheeky grin.

"I'll bring their gear in quickly, and then I must away.
do you think that you will manage them all right?"
says my son. "Anne's operation is scheduled for today
but we won't know any more until tonight."

The children watch him leaving, and they know that something's wrong,
their wide eyes stare at me in sudden fear.
Have they forgotten Granny Seaside? They've been away so long
with their parents in New Zealand for a year.

"It's time for lunch," I tell them, but they just don't want to eat
and nothing that I give them seems to please.
The toys are kicked aside by four uncaring feet,
nor will they climb for comfort on my knees.

I look out of the window at the gloomy, glowering sky,
the sea is smashing, crashing on the sands.
"Come on, let's go exploring, we can't sit here and cry,"
and cocooned in coats, they offer me their hands.

Buffeted by wind-blast and soaked with flying spray
we giggle, struggle out along the beach.
The children shriek with laughter as my hat is blown away
while I keep them cuddled safely within reach.

We storm home, laugh-exhausted, and soon it's time for bed
where, washed and warm, it's 'Granny's Story Time.'
The old, remembered stories, until each drowsy head
sleeps rhythm-soothed and comforted by rhyme.

And now I sit here waiting for the longed-for, dreaded call
that will devastate our lives, or bring us joy.
The sudden ring awakes me, brings me running to the hall.
Thank God! It's all gone well, and it's a boy!

THE PHOTO ALBUM

Thick black covers, heavy paper pages
protecting images of bygone ages.
Photographs carefully annotated,
family events being celebrated.

Grandad and Grandma standing stiff and starchy,
a young lad in uniform – poor Cousin Archie.
Grandma again, look, she's bending to caress
a toddler. Good grief! It's my father in a dress!

Now he's a young man with a lovely grin
mounted on a tandem, going for a spin
with a shy young lady, soon to be his bride.
Here, their wedding photographs, standing side by side.

Groups of all the relatives, look at those huge hats,
one man's even wearing a bowler hat and spats.
That must be Uncle Algie, I remember Aunty Flo
got fed up with his drinking and told him where to go.

Now Mum and Dad are working to set up their own place,
Dad's digging in the garden with a most contented face.
Mum is cutting roses, sniffing every bloom,
you can see she'll soon be joining in the post-war baby boom.

There's my older brother, toddling on a beach
making sure his Mummy is safely within reach.
There's me in a sun hat, and not much else at all —
not the kind of picture to hang up on the wall!

Pictures of more weddings, and then our children too,
grandparents escorting grandchildren to the zoo.
Final loving pictures of parents in old age,
reminders of their courage as they reached the final stage.

Close the thick black covers, and the heavy paper pages,
protecting precious images of bygone ages.
Keep safe the photographs so carefully annotated,
so our children will remember the lives we celebrated.

BIG KISS FOR GRANNY AND GRANDAD

We love our Grand-kids dearly
and though we only stay
roughly six times yearly
as we live so far away,
it's great to take a book or toy
and watch their faces light with joy.

They hurl themselves into our arms,
they love to have a cuddle.
They're good at using all their charms
to get us in a muddle.
"Play this, read that," as on our knees
they climb and give a great big sneeze.

"I love you, Granny, Grandad too,"
as they give a throaty cough.
"Read us another story?"
We want to reply "Gerr-off!"
But what can fond Grandparents do
when faced with kids with incipient 'flu?

So we comfort and cuddle and kiss them,
and help to put them to bed.
Their parents dose them with med'cine
and we all collapse, feeling half-dead.
Now that they all go to school
a 'bug' a week seems to be the rule.

On Sunday night we must return
to our home back in the South,
"Big kiss for Granny, Grandad too,"
with a coughing, slobbery mouth.
I'm sure our children, in their youth,
were so much more infection-proof.

And yes, you've guessed, on our return
we both develop wheezes,
and aching heads that start to burn
and loud, explosive sneezes.
We sniffle and snuffle and loudly complain
but we just can't wait to see them again.

GRANNY GO GO

With five grandchildren growing big and strong
it's difficult to keep up when they come along
to visit their old Granny for a very welcome stay
but I do find it difficult when they want to play.
"Let's go go, Granny, let's go."

They say, "Come on, Granny, kick the ball to me."
So I swing one leg and crack my knee.
The ball goes flying and so do I
and I'm flat on my back gazing up at the sky.
"Oh, no no, Granny, bad show!"

So we take a gentle stroll, a woodland walk,
to educate the darlings with a nature talk
but they have no interest in the birds and the bees
and soon decide they'd rather climb trees.
"Come on, Granny, you're slow!"

So I lift them up to a handy branch
and sit myself down for a picnic lunch.
I eat all of mine and some of theirs as well
but my peaceful moment is shot to hell -
"Granny, Peter's stuck and wants the loo!"

Surprised by my climbing agility
I quickly release them from that tree
only to find, when they're on the ground,
I'm wedged, stuck fast and can't turn around.
"Oh, silly Granny, ho, ho!"

The firemen are really efficient and kind
though convinced I must be out of my mind.
As I'm lowered gently with barely a graze
they thank the grandchildren and load them with praise.
"You're a lucky Granny you know."

The last time they visited the weather was cold
and I was feeling extremely old.
The snow lay deep, nearly topping my hedge,
and the grand-kids proudly showed me their sledge.
"Let's go go, Granny, let's go!"

We wrapped up warm and I took an extra pill
to help me climb up a nearby hill.
"You first, Granny," said Lydia politely,
convinced my attempt was most unlikely.
Suddenly I wanted to go!

I creakily climbed onto that contraption,
I'd show the grand-kids some real action.
They quickly pushed me with a will
and I went careering down that hill.
"Go go, Granny, hooray!"

I swooped and slid, I screamed "Yahoo!"
I showed the grand-kids what to do,
until that very heavy sledge
dumped me in a prickly hedge
where a newsman took a photo.

It was in the papers for all to see,
a snow-white Granny struggling free
from a hedge and a bunch of laughing brats
who'd lost their gloves and lost their hats
as they chased their 'Granny Go Go'.

So now I'll revel in world-wide fame
which goes with my YouTube published name.
I'm 'Granny Go Go' to one and all
but the best is when the grand-kids call
on their lovely 'Granny Go Go'.

NEWTOWN CREEK

Isle of Wight

Through choppy, sideways-sweeping tide,
searching for the guiding mark
to lead us safely deep inside,
we race the ever-deepening dark.

As sunset colours sear the sky
we anchor in the last gold light,
sweet silence broken by the cry
of seabirds settling for the night.

Resting on deck, with drinks in hand,
we await the songs that draw us here –
the magic music from Island land
that floats through Spring-nights every year.

At last, a gentle, warbling starts,
as the nightingales begin their song,
until their music fills our hearts
and lullabies us all night long.

Shakespearean Sonnet

VIEW FROM THE TOP DECK

Looking down from the high top rail
at sullen sea swells rolling by
I watch a yacht with reefed-down sail
defiant against the iron sky.
A shaft of light from the rising sun
reflects in her bow-wave's flashing foam.
She curtseys deep as she tacks to run
for the safety of her harbour home.
The storm's last breath speeds her on her way
as she heads towards the distant shore
and with heavy heart I turn away,
regretting I can sail no more.
Somehow a cruise on this massive ship
cannot compare with a small yacht trip.

THE PEBBLE

Nestled in soft, yielding sand,
back warmed by a water-smoothed rock,
eyes closed against the shimmering sun,
I listened to the sea's soft breathing
whispering, soothing, enticing.

My idly-exploring fingers
found a deep-buried stone which
rolled coolly into my hand, seemingly
of its own will, seeking my touch,
wanting to tell me its story.

Polished by centuries of sea-tumbling,
its strange shape lay in my palm.
One side smooth, rounded,
asking to be caressed and
giving cool comfort in return.

The reverse showed strange hollows
and a deep cleft in which crystals glistened.
Formed by fire and cataclysm,
raised to mountain heights, then crumbled down
by rain and rivers and wind-blown waves.

I could not discard it, leave it there
to be ground down further into sand.
It sits in my bathroom, on a shelf
with sea-shells for company.
As I bathe, I listen again to its story.

TOUGH STUFF

High on the shore a spiky green carpet,
stringy roots deep-grasping the sand,
defying the sea storms.

In sheltering dune shade I lie and listen
to the sighs and whispers of sea and sand,
the gentle rustle of the grass.

But touch its green blades —
here is harsh reality. Like life,
grip it hard and it cuts.

TICKED OFF TWICE (Two trips to hospital)

OPERATION No. 1

Here I lie in a crisp white bed
with pounding heart and aching head
trying wearily to fall asleep
while the dawdling night hours onward creep
and the clock says "Tick".

It hangs on the wall across the room
vaguely gleaming through the gloom.
Grey and round, with electric power
it surely should silently mark the hour
but that clock said "Tick".

No springs and cogs whirling around
to produce a friendly tick-tock sound.
I can't comprehend its noisy ability
to arouse such nervous irritability
each time it says "Tick".

No steady, soothing, heartbeat pace
as the hands traverse its smug, fat face.
A lengthy pause, I start to float,
the clock considers, clears its throat
and says "Tick!"

Muted voices, measured tread,
nurses moving round my bed.
"Other patients resting deep,
please, do try and get to sleep,"
and the clock said "Tick!"

Each disturbing whip-crack sound
picks me up and spins me round.
A pause, a silence, is it dead?
No - for pounding through my head
the clock says "TICK!"

I start to count the lapse between
Each "tick" from creeping hands unseen.
Ninety seconds? - I'm too weary
to contemplate Einstein's famous theory
as the clock goes "TICK!"

Has Earth-time slowed as here I lie?
Is my soul now soaring into the sky?
Did the clock slow my heartbeat 'til I'm dead
helpless, defenceless in my bed?
"HA HA" said the clock - "T I C K!"

OPERATION No. 2

Back again in a hospital bed
I hear once more the sound I dread.
That hospital clock high on the wall
is even worse than I recall —
it still says "Tick".

Last time I had a single room
I hadn't notice in the gloom
the clock that, in the quiet of night,
would suddenly wake me with a fright
when it said "Tick".

Not "Tick, tock, tick" with friendly pace,
comforting in this dreadful place.
No! This clock wants to drive me mad,
it doesn't care if I feel bad
when it says "Tick".

The thing's electric, for God's sake!
So why does it keep me awake
by shouting in its scratchy way
all night and on into the day
with its nasty "Tick"?

The surgeon soon will come for me
to operate upon my knee.
I've had no sleep, I'm scared and sick —
perhaps if I am very quick?
"No!" said the clock. "Sit!"

I'm wheeled away, the job is done
before I had a chance to run.
So now, confined, back in my bed
again comes echoing through my head
that bloody tick!

I’m sure that it is louder now
that I am helpless, in its power.
I scream, a nurse comes running quick,
asks me if I’m feeling sick.
“That clock said tick!”

“Yes, dear, clocks usually do that.”
(Thinking ‘What a silly old bat!’)
She turns on the professional charm
and smiling says, “There is no harm
in just a tick.”

“It’s just a clock, that’s all my dear,
there really is nothing to fear.”
They give me pills and tuck me in,
the clock looks down, and with a grin
says “TICK!”

That’s it, it really is too bad,
the clock is driving me quite mad.
I’m off the bed and in my clutch
I have a strong and weighty crutch.
I’ll give it stick!

My knee is healed, but not my mind,
and though the staff in here are kind
they really do not understand
that I cannot control my hand
when a clock says “Tick”.

So now I’m not allowed to roam
freely round my nice ‘care home’.
They shut me in, I can’t be trusted
since every clock I find gets busted
and can’t go tick.

But tonight my window’s open wide,
they’ll not keep me locked up inside!
I’m off to London to see Big Ben
and save the world at midnight when
BIG BEN GOES TICK!

(Exits through window with crutch and manic laughter.)

THE SEA HORSE

Out of the mist he came
dancing, prancing.
Onto the beach he came,
strange, entrancing
steed with shining, silver hide,
nostrils blowing fierce and wide,
full of joy and fire and pride.

Into the mist he flew,
dancing, prancing.
Kicking up sand he flew,
briefly glancing
with eyes the colour of the sea
before he turned and ran from me,
foam-flecked white mane flying free.

Tendrils of mist began
rising, swirling.
Sea-scented mist began
skywards curling.
On the shore, no horse in sight,
Only hoof prints, filled with light-
reflecting sea-foam, creamy white.

IN TRAINING

In swirling Autumn breeze,
caressed by flying colours
tossed down by waving trees,
I thunder past the others.

Strong-willed, and very green,
fierce-fighting for his head,
so obviously keen
to prove how well he's bred

the new boy in my stable
burns up the practice track
and I doubt that I'll be able
to stop and turn him back.

At last, his mouth responding,
he comes back to my hand
and I pray that I am bonding
with the best horse in the land.

So many things could stop us
from achieving racing fame,
an accident, a virus,
or a bruise to make him lame.

Whatever lies before him
I know we'll never part,
for this fiery-coloured flyer
is burnt into my heart.

ON THE FIRST DAY

Floating, gliding, smooth and supple,
arched neck bowing to my demands,
your soft mouth gently responding.
I ask extension, feel surging power,
steel muscles under velvet skin.
Steady now, steady now!

Into canter, flying changes,
piaffe, passage and pirouette,
half-pass with calm elegance,
canter, circle, then centre line
to halt and proudly salute.
Well done, well done!

Tomorrow we will fly,
facing the challenges you love
as we hurtle across country.
Free to release your power,
the fire within that knows no fear,
you'll have my trust.

On the third day, our final test.
Once more, control must play a part
while aching muscles must respond
to clear each jump, then twist and turn,
accelerate for the final burn, for
Gold, Olympic Gold!

Petrarchan Sonnet

EN GARDE

The fencers raise their weapons in salute,
young lads now facing their first testing day.
The taller, trembling, eager for the fray,
his rival calmer, seeming more astute.
The referee, a man of great repute,
calls 'En garde, are you ready? Play!'
Their blades engage, athletic bodies sway,
attack, riposte – the watching crowd is mute.
Experience wins, defeating height and reach
but each has somehow gained more skill today
to face whatever future fortune brings.
I pray that no real conflict comes to teach
these young men how to kill the modern way
where bombs and guns replace the blade that sings.

FLAT FISH

Flat fish are despondent
and this is the reason why
they grovel in the gravel
while other fish swim by.

They're hatched with eyes opposing
but one eye walks around
'til the youngster feels unbalanced
and falls flat on the ground.

Now one side is its topside
and t'other's down below
so it flops and flaps and flounders
and just can't seem to go.

While other fish fly past him
with flashing silvery sides
the Flat Fish changes colour
and, drifting downwards, hides.

But when the Sharks are hunting
or the Dolphins dashing by,
the Flat Fish, sunk in sand below,
stays put - and winks his eye!

A Villanelle

A SILLY 'VILLY'

If I could write a Villanelle
would you publish it one day?
I'd really do it very well.

My heart with pride would surely swell
if I could only hear you say
that I could write a Villanelle.

I'd punctuate with care, and spell
the Oxford dictionary way.
I'd really do it very well.

I'd struggle on through weeks of hell,
I'd even humbly kneel and pray
for help to write a Villanelle.

The years go by, and I can tell
it's rather futile now to say
I'd really do it very well.

As I await my death-bed knell
I seem to hear from far away
"Yes, she did write a Villanelle –
she really did it very well!"

A Villanelle

A FOND FAREWELL

I'm leaving now, I'm going far away,
our partnership is coming to an end
although you said you wanted me to stay.

I think, you dog, you've really had your day.
Those loving e-mails that your girlfriends send
have pissed me off, I'm going far away.

Look at this one, from tarty, smarty Fay,
the girl you told me was an old school friend
and I believed you wanted me to stay.

I'll not hang round until I'm old and grey
in hope that you your wicked ways will mend,
I'm leaving now, I'm going far away.

Don't even try explaining yesterday,
your lying words have sent me round the bend
although you said you wanted me to stay.

I can't believe a single word you say
I'm telling you at last that I intend
to leave you now, I'm going far away
although you said you wanted me to stay.

Shakespearean Sonnet

THE HILL FARM

I rest against the rusty farmyard gate
to watch the dawn discovering the hills.
A blackbird sings a love-song to his mate
with soaring, long arpeggios and trills
as morning mist drifts up the mountain side
and grazing cows emerge through swirls of white.
A pheasant barks then creeps away to hide
in woodland safe from foxes' slit-eyed sight.
At last the sun drinks up the rising mist,
great, rocky crags reach up against the sky,
and now, unveiled, my sheep appear pink-kissed
by sunbeams as the new day draws them high.
My life is tied to these demanding lands
but age will pass them soon to younger hands.

I CRY FOR THE MOUNTAINS

I cry for the mountains – the day's now long past
since I answered their call. The shadows they cast
spread chilly despair through my heart and my soul.
My life has no meaning. My life has no goal.

I dream of the mountains at night in my sleep,
of the mornings I wandered alone with the sheep,
the mist soft, caressing, the heather in bloom –
and then I awaken back here in this room.

I'm old and I'm crippled and always in pain
and I know I will never go climbing again,
but Oh! God in Heaven! Is it very wrong
to long for the days when my muscles were strong?

When I strode up the trackways, content and alone,
the peaks would embrace me and make me their own.
I was one with the mountains, their breeze was my breath,
no thought then of old age, of illness and death.

The pleasure of testing my youth and my strength
in wild, windy weather to travel the length
of ridges and corries, escarpment and crown,
to stand on the summit, a king looking down!

I know I'm an old man, and should be content
to remember the wonderful days that I spent
walking high in the hill tops, not dulled with despair.
I cry for the mountains, stuck here in my chair.

Cinquain

SHEPHERD'S WARNING

Scarlet
tipped with bright gold
morning clouds writhe upwards
writing a warning in the sky
a storm.

HAVEN

Silence
peaceful haven
impossible to find
in our modern, busy cities.
Mountain.

FIRST LOVE

Perfume
softly wafting
into the still, night air.
sad memories of long-lost love,
regrets.

HAIKU

Soft snow and silence
blue shadows in cold moonlight,
a new baby's cry.

Young lovers embrace
blossom petals bless their heads,
sinking evening sun.

May-time's silver song
worshipping the rising moon,
secret nightingale.

Ripples in dark pool
dance with crystals of blue sky,
flash of kingfisher.

COMING HOME

Driving home, relaxed from lazy days
in Suffolk's peaceful, reed-filled lands
where the curlew warbles his haunting cry
and the elegant avocet sifts the sands,
we stopped for lunch at Alton.

Strangely busy, the streets were filled
with remnants of a welcome-home parade.
Young soldiers in desert fatigues strolled by
surrounded by families no longer afraid
their sons would not come home.

But their faces still showed memories
of the searing heat of desert war
and thoughts of friends who would not return
to the chilly British Autumn shore.
How could they explain?

Warm in a hotel dining room,
in a circle of friends, six camouflaged boys
smiled with sad mouths, their eyes far away,
while the youngest, shivering, merely toyed
with the dull, inedible food.

We know they are brave, these newly-made men,
they did all that could be expected out there,
but at what lasting cost to their young lives?
Across the noisy, crowded room a pair
of horror-haunted eyes gazed into mine –

and I wept for my son.

IS THERE ANYBODY THERE?

I sit in the darkness,
the damp, and the cold,
alone with my loneliness ...
Is there anybody there?

A blanket round my back,
and blankness in my mind,
no home to call my own ...
but does anybody care?

A church porch for my bed,
the main door locked and barred,
Should I kneel down and pray?
Is there anybody there?

Inspired by NSPCC Advertisement

ALONE

Dark, limpid eyes, full of shadows and pain,
brimming with unshed tears,
haunted by terrible fears,
calling, calling in vain.
Hungry and cold, the little boy stands,
gripping cot bars with his trembling hands …
but Mummy has gone out again.

BALLERINA

Delicate hands lifted high,
fingers in classical pose,
arms soft, boneless –
wafting like willow fronds.

Head poised on long neck,
hair in controlled chignon.
Expression aloof, yet sometimes
melting into gentle sadness.

Body pliant, always young,
carried on shapely limbs
slender as a gazelle's,
with smooth, steel muscles.

Heart totally enslaved by her art,
soul controlled by music's demands.
A whole, short lifetime of pain,
hard work, and ecstasy.

Now, old and stiff and tired,
enfolded in rug-strewn chair,
classic music surrounds her ...
and her soul still dances.

NIGHT LIGHTS

Darkness, no moon tonight,
no distracting noise.
The village lies wrapped in a soft blanket of sleep
while silent owls dream
in the ivy-clad oak.

Heavy with tiredness, I turn off the light
and lie in my warm, comfortable bed
longing for that swift oblivion,
that descent into dreams,
that now I rarely achieve.

Suddenly, my legs move,
walking me awake.
Pain stabs through nerves like attacking insects,
biting here, stinging there,
buzzing in my brain.

Light back on,
I read until my weary eyes start to close
then turn off the light, but not my brain
which clamours for attention
like a spoilt child.

On goes the light again — a trip to the bathroom —
back to bed, light off. No good,
I need the comfort of a cuppa,
so on goes the light and the kettle.
Extinguish light, cover my head.

My home is a lighthouse, flashing its warning
"Danger! Old wreck lies here!"
Around me, neighbours sleep on in their darkness,
no windows morse-coding replies to my signals.

FLYING DUTCHMAN SYNDROME

Strange, how slowly the moonlit night
saunters by with leisured pace,
averting her star-gaze from the sight
of salt tears streaming down my face.

No rest for me, racked by the curse
of restless legs and nerves on fire.
I pace the floor, composing verse
while the cold-faced moon climbs ever higher.

It seems there is no medication
to cure this 'Flying Dutchman' disease
so I walk in search of inspiration
like that mariner ever roaming the seas.

Nowhere to rest, too tired to think,
words waft away and out of sight.
The uncaring moon begins to sink
into the pink-tinged morning light.

Strange, how short the night time seems
when the sun revives the dawning day,
scattering bird song with his beams,
chasing the weary night away.

No time to rest, no chance to sleep,
the daylight hours go hurrying past.
All thoughts of verse will have to keep
until my family sleeps at last.

Strange, how fast the daylight hours
rush to join the sinking sun.
Bird song stops and fading flowers
bow to a new night just begun.

Exhausted now, I try to sleep,
dozing fitfully for a while,
but soon the Dutchman comes to keep
me company every weary mile.

Strange, how my lifetime rushes by,
without a single chance to express
my inner soul, my heartfelt cry —
will my poetry ever achieve success?

LOSING IT

Memories of laughing friends,
days out by the sea,
and here's a card from John, who sends
'Get Well Soon' to me.
Who's he?

It was on holiday, I know,
I met my handsome Fred.
We danced, and watched a theatre show,
and very soon were wed.
Dear Fred.

But that was many years ago,
I wonder where he's gone?
Now I live on my own, although
I think I have a son
called John.

A lady comes in every day;
she's fun and full of laughter
I feel sad when she goes away —
she looks just like my daughter
Elaine.

Who are these people round my bed?
Fred, tell them to go away!
And what was that Elaine just said?
"She's losing it today."
No way!

Where is this place? Is that you, Fred?
Are we on holiday?
I really thought that you were dead,
you've been so long away.
Please stay.

Why, dear Elaine and darling John,
how nice of you to call.
Oh, it's a nurse and Doctor Brown.
You say I had a fall?
I don't recall.

HOLDING ON

Windows fastened tight,
heavy curtains drawn,
keeping out the world,
the glaring, busy world,
holding you here with me.

I fumble in darkness
where shadows cast your form
in your favourite chair. Then
upstairs, familiar footsteps tread
and a silent door shuts.

The insistent phone
clamours and calls
while neighbours knock
reminding me that you have gone.
I close my ears.

In our dark house, quietly
your presence surrounds me.
My love holds you safe
as I smell your clothes
and hear your laugh.

With no faith to save you
how can I let you go?
How can I follow
if I don't know
where you've gone?

SEARCHING THE MIST

Cool caress of mist,
dampness defining trees and shadows
in my world of dreams and despair.

Our special path shifts
from known to mysterious.
A new world, insubstantial.

Seeking our favourite hill
my mist-filled eyes betray
my floundering footsteps

until I stand, confused,
reaching out a hand
to touch the memory of you.

STAR GAZING

Standing alone on a still, velvet night,
a gentle wind whispering by,
I'm completely entranced by the glorious sight
of so many stars piercing the sky.

How tiny our Earth, how pathetically small
is this globe where we struggle to live
through famine and warfare, ignoring the call
to share and conserve, to love and forgive.

Each country develops some form of belief,
saying 'This is the God to believe in'.
Their fanatical rules bring nothing but grief
and more wars in the name of religion.

Stop, look at the sky, feel the wonder and awe
as constellations wheel by overhead.
Supernovae explode, and then millions more
earth planets are formed in their stead.

Are there other life forms that have found a way
to live without anger or strife?
Have they found their own God, so that every day
they peacefully follow their life?

It's beyond understanding, too huge for my mind,
this universe whirling through space.
I pray that one day all Earth's people will find
that their God may reveal His true face

Lightning Source UK Ltd.
Milton Keynes UK
UKOW05f2357270317
297664UK00001B/4/P